# Plumber Paige
## Let's Fix a Running Toilet

By: Paige Knowles

This book is dedicated to:

My sisters for always loving and supporting me!

# Hi!

## My name is Plumber Paige

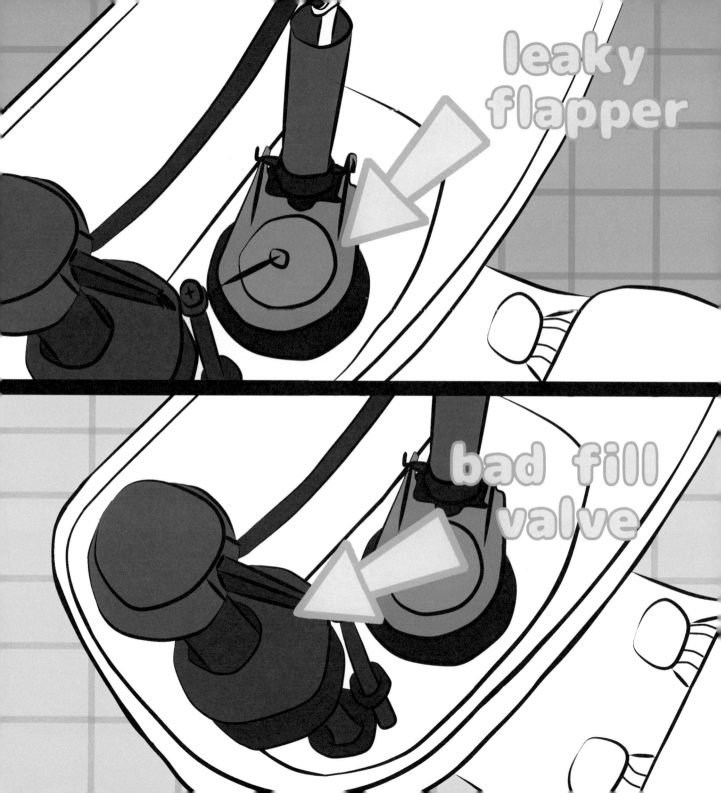

# Today, we are going to replace both.

This is what we will need:

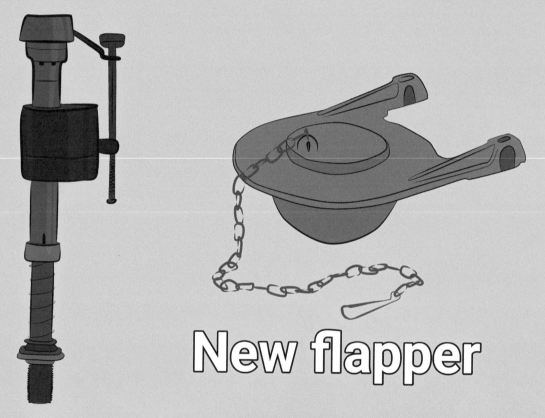

New fill valve

New flapper

# Step One:

## Start by shutting off the water to the toilet.

Flush the toilet to get as much of the water out as you can.

# Step Three:

## Loosen and take off the nut and supply line from the fill valve.

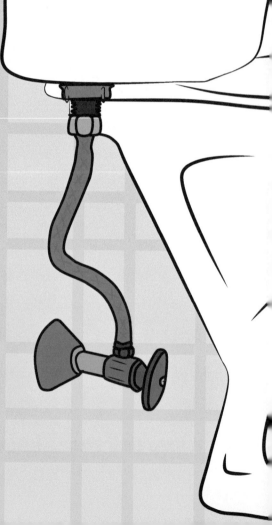

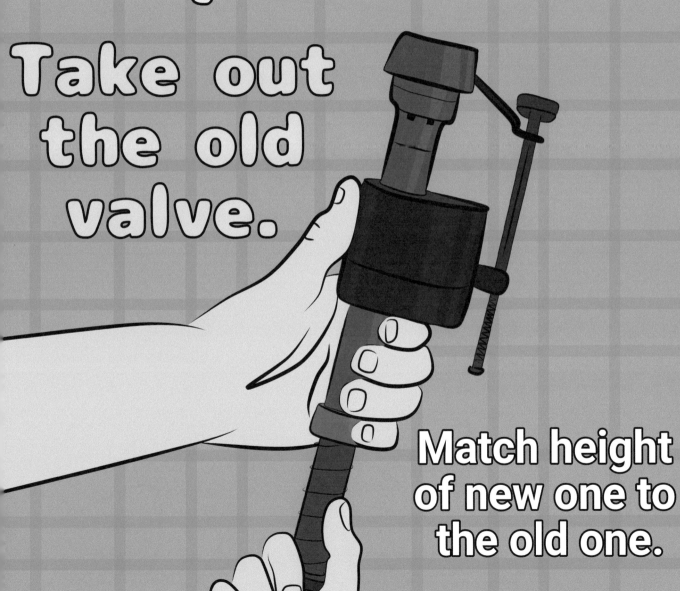

# Step Seven:

## Attach the new flapper. Adjust the chain length.

**Tip:** The flapper should lift when the handle is pushed.

Nothing should leak and the running should have stopped.

# To fix a running toilet...

**1st:** Turn off the water and hold down the handle.

**2nd:** Empty the tank.

**3rd:** Take off supply line and nut from the fill valve.

**4th:** Match height of old and new fill valve.

**5th:** Put in new valve and tighten with nut.

**6th:** Unhook chain and take out old flapper.

**7th:** Attach new flapper. Adjust chain length.

**8th:** Put the supply line back on.

**Lastly:** Turn on and check for leaks.

# About the Author

## Paige  Knowles

Paige Knowles is a trades advocate and public speaker, as well as a new business owner (Plumber Paige LLC). Since graduating from the plumbing and heating lab in high school, she has enrolled in a local community college for construction management. Her goal is to end the stigma around the construction industry and get more people to consider a career in the skilled trades. She does this by creating books like this one, telling students they can do jobs like these. Paige also works closely with Let's Build Construction Camp for Girls and is starting to expand her reach all over the world

(Learn more about Let's Build Construction Camp for Girls at letsbuildcamp.com)

Find out more on Paige and how you can support her mission on her website: plumberpaige.com or follow her on social media!

Plumber Paige - YouTube

Instagram- plumber _paige

Plumber Paige - Facebook

Tik Tok - plumber _paige

plumber _paige - Twitter

# Disclaimer:

This is not the only way to fix a running toilet. There may be other problems, these are just the most common. Contact a professional plumber if you need guidance on this job. Find a follow-along video on the Plumber Paige YouTube channel.

# Glossary:

**Flush Valve** - Valve located in the center of tank. Has a hole where the water flows from the tank into the bowl when the toilet is flushed.

**Fill Valve** - This valve brings water into the tank when the water level lowers, until it is refilled.

**Flapper** - Rubber seal that sits on the flush valve. It is connected to the flush lever by chain and lifts to allow water to escape the tank.